# THE
# MONEY
# PHENOMENON

# THE
# MONEY
# PHENOMENON

## *A Concise Introduction To What Money Is*

### *Louis Russell*

Aoriston™

aoriston.net

ISBN: 9781792742835

# DEDICATION

τοῖς ἀγγέλοις τοῖς ζωοῖς ἤ τεθνεῶσι

# CONTENTS

# ACKNOWLEDGMENTS

Had a handful of teachers over the years neglected to answer the call, the substance of this book could have scarcely been thought, let alone recorded.

# INTRODUCTION

This is a little book about money. It's also a book about being human. It is a guide that attempts to dissolve the fog of mystery that surrounds money, which can prevent societies and individuals within them from realizing their full potential.

This is not a book about investing strategies. This is not a book about ways to get rich quick. It will not teach you how to escape yourself. Its concern is more basic than quantitative analysis. Its purpose is to purify the most interesting and useful ideas of major economic theorists and then to bring those ideas to bear on the social reality.

Money is a mystery to us: we use it fluently, but we actually know very little *about* it. How can we thoughtlessly use an instrument so often yet devote so little thought to the mechanics that underlie it? We do think about money, of course. But there is a difference between the thought that *money is a thing* and the thought **that** *there is a thing called money*.

All subsequent chapters of this book scarcely, if ever, use the personal pronoun 'I'. But this book is the product of my having graduated from college in 2010 during the throes of a major credit contraction. The Silicon Valley, which had just undergone the bursting of the tech bubble, was now forced to come to grips with the second major economic crisis of that decade.

Even as an economics major, I hadn't fully grasped the effects that the collapse of the housing bubble had had on my job prospects. In order to be hired, especially at a startup, an employee had to come screaming out of the womb adding immediate, measurable value.

It is necessary not only for individuals, but also for societies to come to grips with a sound understanding of what money is—or, more accurately, how it works, because money is by no means reducible to the physical paper on which it is printed.

What began as an autobiographical account of my thought processes and experiences concerning money slowly evolved into a deep curiosity to understand how money works as a technology, and, more importantly, what people can do with that knowledge. The chain of events, which began with the credit collapse of 2007-8 and ended with me back at my parents' home after a wild, three year run in graduate school, gave me the tools I would need to sustain a legitimate interrogation of economic theory.

In retracing my steps, I can see that the residual impact of the financial crisis *forced* me to look for a more grounded solution than a 'career', because no career at that time was legitimately stable. Even established engineers were overworked and constantly looking for ways out of the feedback loop of a 'normal' job. I decided that, if the adult life of the average American not born independently wealthy consisted of being forced into a long-term suicide in the form of extreme hours and unnecessary stress, I would at least die trying to enrich myself.

I eventually received an education sufficient to propel me past the entry-level phase of my employment. But, in taking a risk for the sake of my future, I had taken out student loans to finance the entire enterprise. Oops. *Oopsies.* I hadn't ever needed to come to terms with money on a philosophical level. And why do so? For years I could simply swipe my credit card or sign a promissory note and be well on my way toward the life I wanted. At last, the day came when I could no longer maintain the illusion that money didn't matter.

I had become dissociated from my financial self on a quest for a spiritual knowledge that I couldn't define. This led to a monetary meltdown. I could no longer adhere to the rack-it-up-now-and-worry-later mentality. I could no longer swipe credit cards whimsically and shred the bills as they came. The mass of the negative balance eventually began to threaten my life and my health. I could no longer refuse to acknowledge it. Moreover, the question demanded to be answered: what is money? Why has it mastered me? Most importantly, how can *I* master *it*?

I don't have a fixed philosophy for how every person other than me ought to live their lives. But I do believe that transmuting moments of suffering into positive experiences and knowledge can serve as a guiding candle to sustain lifelong inquisitiveness. By naming and confronting the deepest sources of my pain and deprivation, first by my want of an education, second by the need for money that the desire for that education at any cost has produced, I have tapped into a seemingly inexhaustible source of inspiration that has propelled me on a wild ride through the last decade of my life. Of course, I could have at any moment let the waves of fear and shame govern my decisions.

My quest for a form of life that I was comfortable calling 'fulfilling' led me to wind up, at the age of 27, face down on the carpet of the bedroom I had spent my teenage years sleeping in. I had thoroughly exhausted myself in pursuit of the education I had set out for, and now I was feeling crushed beneath the weight of a series of student loans I had stacked to the ceiling. But this was only terrifying because I hadn't thought about my situation carefully. My anxiety about how I would 'pay it all back' was pointing me into more chaos. I cried out, I clenched my fist, I pounded my desk. But those angsty moments in the mirror or laying on a carpet were alone worth it all. In losing my sense of self-respect that I had convinced myself was tied to a dollar amount, I *found* something I didn't know that I had been looking for. For the first time in a long time, I started to laugh. I laughed long and hard. Why had I been in flight?

In that laughter, my vision opened up. I suddenly had space—I could *breathe* again. Like when I was younger, before I had felt such heavy anxiety. Some part of me had finally stopped running. In that joy, I became able to sit calmly in the presence of the deeper truths from which I had been turning away. I have done my best to translate these ineffable lessons into intelligible language, all within the context of philosophy, philology, and especially economics.

In the couple years since I began to reflect on my relationship to myself, to money, and how it mediates my relationship to society, I have seen my hourly income increase six-fold. I went from working dead-end jobs to becoming self-employed in a profession I loved, was proud of, and *was good at*.

But these changes did not happen overnight. Moreover, they were only made possible by means of discarding disordered thought patterns for healthier and more stable approaches. Only by walking through the shame, anger, and terror of having made dreadful errors did the process of changing become first possible, then actual. I had to define my problem, feel my emotions, and learn to trust my understanding. My problem had to do with money—that much I understood. I suspected that I needed more of it. But it became clearer and clearer that I didn't understand *what money is*.

Money as a pure concept is much more durable than coins and paper. But you already know this. If money were simply a physical object, then it would be easy to come by. Moreover, no human mind would be required to determine what counts as money and what doesn't. In endlessly repeating that we want more money, there is great confusion about what we actually want more of, not to mention the limits of money to provide it.

I've designed this book to be crucial. It covers the complex philosophical and economic ideas of thinkers ranging from Aristotle to Minsky in colloquial, American English that is intended to give my readers access to their fundamental insights without requiring a doctoral dissertation to do so. It would be a challenge to understate the importance of developing a sound understanding of these topics. Make a little space—that's all this book needs.

Nobody requires a financial crisis to understand that money is fundamental to the life of every person. This essay is short, sweet, and directly to the point. While money is not a deity and does not guarantee happiness, thinking about money superficially almost always engenders misery. Having more money can only enhance one's possibilities on the surface level of human existence. In order to allow money to work in the context of a human life, there is a more fundamental battle that must be won: this is, as Plato puts it, the victory over the self.

I have told you about how the asking of this simple question changed my life. If you have made it this far, maybe you are curious, or maybe you have the inkling that this little essay can help you. Because money is so fundamental to human societies, a healthy understanding of money is rudimentary to a healthy way of life. I have designed this book in order to help increase the spectrum of my reader's knowledge in order to produce an understanding of money both up close and in context.

This book aims at the metaphysical level of scientific knowledge about money. The idea will be to operate on a more fundamental plane of thought about money rather than to coach readers on the specifics of who they should be. While future works may engage in detailed ways to generate income and how to navigate political systems, this work strives for fundamental truths about money as a means of exchange, as capital, and as credit.

The need for change presents itself most obviously during moments of collapse. While I consider the low points I went through in some sense precious as learning experiences, why wait for actual desolation to prepare for its looming possibility? Wherever you are in your thought process, this book will help you build a sound conceptual foundation for thinking about money that will help you meet your personal challenges. But no book, no teacher, no school of thought can meet those challenges for you. This book is not simply about money, but about being human. Healthy management of resources lies at the center of that enterprise.

But the styles with which people govern their lives depend on their personal contexts and values. The word 'freedom' means different things to different people. This book isn't designed to define what that term means for every person, but to help every person discover what financial freedom means for him or herself.

# PROLOGUE

S mith, Marx, Simmel, et al. put forth the basic notion that money is not an object but a dynamic pivot point facilitative of trade—by serving as a measure of the value of commodities, money makes trade simple and easy. Nigel Dodd has recently presented an account of monetary theory in his The Social Life of Money, which takes a brute force approach toward decoding various thematic aspects of what money is. Careful study of these works calls for career-long academic dedication, not a mere weekend perusal.

Yet the problems that Americans and many more face concern not just academics and economic decision makers, but also the people who deal every day in the currencies and values in question. This work, by no means exhaustive, condenses several of the most interesting and applicable perspectives from the work of numerous scholars into intelligible moments that will orient the reader as to current points of view on the topic. I have done my best to cite as many sources and passages as possible so that the dedicated reader can do more detailed research than is fitting for this work, which ultimately wants to get back to what these theories mean *for specific people in the present moment.*

# CHAPTER ONE

## *Medium Of Exchange And Measure Of Value*

Let's briefly consider some fundamental notions in philosophy before we break into the topic of this chapter. The Greek word for 'commodity' is chrēma (χρῆμα). This noun derives from the verb *chraōmai* (χράομαι), which means 'I use'. The two basic functions of commodities are use and exchange. We find this distinction in Aristotle, who distinguishes the two functions of commodities with the example of a pair of shoes: a person can either use the pair of shoes by wearing them or trade the shoes for something else.[1] Both applications of a commodity are uses of it, but one way of using the commodity inheres in the ultimate purpose of the thing itself, and the other puts the commodity to work for the sake of obtaining some

---

1: Arist.Pol. I.3.11, 1257a9-14, Trans. Rackham. 'Take for example a shoe—there is its wear as a shoe and there is its use as an article of exchange; for both are ways of using a shoe, inasmuch as even he that barters a shoe for money or food with the customer that wants a shoe uses it as a shoe, though not for the use peculiar to a shoe, since shoes have not come into existence for the purpose of barter.'

other commodity. Even if a cobbler makes a pair of shoes for the purpose of selling them, he ultimately makes shoes that can be worn. The Greek vocabulary preserves the sense that a proper commodity is to be used rather than exchanged.

This fundamental Aristotelian distinction helps Smith, Marx, and others distinguish between *use value* and *exchange value*. The use value of a commodity is the value a person receives from consuming or using that commodity on their own; the exchange value is the commodity's value in an exchange of goods. Money is a special commodity, because its use value is its value in exchange. Both applications—use and exchange—are *uses* of commodities, but they are different *types* of uses. Money defies this logic, because *its very purpose is to be exchanged*.

Immanuel Kant makes several useful innovations on basic Aristotelian philosophy. Aristotle observes that a quantity always accompanies an intellection of a quantitative object.[2] Kant expands on this necessity by supplying the notion of transcendental apperception as

---

2: Arist.DM. I, 450a1-4ff., Trans. Bloch. 'for the same affection that occurs in drawing a diagram also occurs in thinking: for when drawing a diagram we make no use of the fact that the quantity of the triangle drawn is determinate, but still we draw it as having a determinate quantity; and similarly a person who thinks, even if he does not think about a quantity, he posits a quantity before his eyes, but does not think about it as a quantity...' The sense is that a quantitative analytic inheres in the object of thought.

the conditions of possibility for thought and experience. The 'I think' synthesizes intuitions and concepts into the scientific possibility of experiential understanding. This sounds complex and abstract, but it simply means that the individual always experiences the physical world in terms of space and time (intuitions). As space and time are being experienced, the mind synthesizes the physical world into knowledge by means of various categories that the world draws into play (categories). These pure concepts are still quite abstract—let's make them crystal clear with our prior example of a shoe.

In the same moment that I see a shoe, I see the shoe as *one* shoe. I can imagine other shoes, but this shoe is a quantity of one (concept of magnitude). This is the concept of unity that the world of experience draws into play *while I look at the shoe.* Further, because I see the shoe and I'm reasonably certain that I am not dreaming and haven't been drugged, I am sure that this is a *real* shoe that will persist for a determinate period of time (concept of reality). Of course, one shoe alone is hardly useful. The sight of the shoe always causes me to think about where the other shoe might be (concept of causality). Perhaps my dog likes to run off with these shoes in particular, which causes me to think about my dog running through the house with the shoe in its mouth. Now, there are more of these pure concepts, but you get the idea. The experiential world draws these concepts into play, and even in this simple example we see that these concepts allow us to navigate the world with something very much like knowledge. This applies to money directly, because the Kantian model shows us a possible way of explaining how we make sense of the world. But let's now ground ourselves in our discussion of money.

We have seen that the mind cannot help but apply a magnitude or quantity to the physical objects that it experiences or considers. Kojin Karatani observes that the transcendental apperceiver, the 'self' that blends intuitions and concepts into experience and understanding, necessarily synthesizes every commodity into an *exchange value*. This allows us to understand every exchangeable commodity in terms of its price. A monetary quantity rather amazingly accounts for the total reality of the commodity. By honest reflection on the pervasive 'bottom line' mentality, we witness the truth of Unamuno's statement that markets tend to flatten *every object* into a quantity in economic space and time—that is, we give *everything* an easily intelligible price. The mere presence of a physical object—*any* physical object, says Unamuno—pulls into play the varied conceptual and intuitive apparatus by which we determine price. We can put a label on it and measure it by its economic value. The money commodity, which is an abstract mathematical representation of a complex synthesis, has the capacity to ascribe a dollar amount to nearly *anything*. This is what we mean by referring to the money commodity as the *measure of value*.

Money as a measure of value determines the quantity of commodities by labeling each commodity with a price. But we will get ourselves into trouble should we neglect to observe an Aristotelian distinction that Hume translates into English as 'matters of fact' and 'relations of ideas'. Every priced object exists within a set of obscenely complex circumstances. The price of the object is contingent upon the features of its dynamic and diverse environment.

This means that space and time always factor into the pricing of the commodity. We see an example of this at sporting events, airports, or other places in circumstances where vendors charge extreme rates for beverages that would otherwise cost 10 percent of the price. Although it is represented as a mathematical quantity, price is of course an *extremely* dynamic measurement that is continuously correcting itself in light of new information. My basic meaning is that the same object cannot have a single value, but has different values for different people, in different places, and at different times. This variability leads to imprecision in determining price, because market actors have imperfect information. The inaccuracy of the market accounts for how day-traders and investors can make a living by predicting these inaccuracies. But the natural tendency is to ignore the extreme complexity and variations in price and to view it as the final say on the 'value' of an object.

The term economics derives from the Ancient Greek word *oikonomia* (οἰκονομία), which basically means the governance of a household. *Chrematismos* (χρηματισμός), on the other hand, is purely the art of making money. *Chrematismos* is a necessary skill. Aristotle viewed business dealings as the necessary but non-exhaustive means to a more expansive self-fulfillment—that is, generating enough income is a necessary requirement for a happy life, but in no way ensures happiness. Georg Simmel observes that money as a means of exchange breaches this boundary and tends to absorb all physical or even non-physical objects into the impersonal, scientific, and objective rationality that appropriates all phenomena into economic quantities.

Money as a means of exchange continually threatens to reduce *everything* to a price for which any component of human society—including the people themselves—can in one way or another be packaged into a quantity and exchanged. This causes some philosophers to panic, others to celebrate. But no economic quantity can absolutely represent any entity in its full context. No matter what an economic value is said to represent, price is almost always a distorted and fanatical way of representing any object *in the long run*. Yet even conspicuously absurd prices or economic arrangements that are bound to collapse in the long run may long outlive the human being who recognizes this absurdity. This is why timing is so crucial for financial speculation.

The ambiguous meaning of the word *value* may call to mind either an economic or a moral value. A person uses their moral values as a compass by which they determine right from wrong. In the economic sense, commodities have both a use value and an exchange value. Adam Smith and Karl Marx liked to think of history as an arithmetic progression of time from one point to the next. This problematic but commonsense way of thinking often leads to a lamenting of the debauched present in favor of the much nobler past. It seems to many people that all commodities ought to be useful in some morally obvious way.

Aristotle viewed money as unnatural, because the paper or metal on which it is printed has nothing near the value that the note or coin does. Norman O. Brown captures this line of reasoning when he says that the essence of money is pure fancy and absolute irrationality. We can take Aristotle and Brown to mean that the physical object of which money is made has no immediately recognizable purpose. Without the human society to support money as the means of exchange, it would have no use. Money as a measure of value elevates this absurdity to a higher pitch by giving this apparently useless commodity the power to measure the value of *all other commodities*.

Adam Smith reflects meaningfully on why the money commodity has its value. He first points out that the thorough division of labor necessitates a medium of exchange between traders who produce diverse products and have various needs. The product of the specialized worker can only supply a limited part of their wants. This worker will require a way to trade with others who manufacture the items they require for survival, but which they do not themselves produce. In the absence of money, any trade between producers requires that every trader locate another trader who both has precisely what they need and needs precisely what they have.

Few literate cultures ever suffered through this primitive and inefficient method of trading. The Mycenaeans developed their early alphabet 'Linear B' as a tool to track economic transactions over three thousand years ago. Smith notes that Romans invented metal coinage to address the challenges that finding a mutually suitable trade presents.

With coinage, every highly specialized trader can accept and pay in money (medium of exchange) for a certain amount thereof (measure of value) rather than in a particular commodity for which there is variable demand. Today, I can pay a farmer cash for a basket of blueberries rather than persuade him to trade me the blueberries for an .epub of my latest essay. Paper money or debit cards linked to electronic banking systems currently operate as the fundamental media that make possible transactions between buyers and sellers with extreme variations in their needs and specializations. Efficient trade simply requires a medium to which traders can turn to complete their transactions. The money commodity is of course this medium of exchange. A person's net worth can be thought of as a sort of percentage ownership of the national 'market cap'.

We have also earlier appropriated Smith's term measure of value.3 Some quantity of the money commodity stands in perpetual relation to the value of the given commodity in the marketplace. The basic model for understanding price is the supply and demand curve. If Thales corners the market for olive oil, he has the power to raise the prices as high as he would like. If there are many producers, this will drive the price down. Buyers and sellers alike think of all marketplace commodities in terms of these price quantities. Any purchase or sale clearly requires an agreed upon price.

Every commodity commands a certain price or a certain quantity of money in a marketplace transaction. The commodity's price acts as a placeholder for that commodity's exchange value. For Smith, the socially necessary labor time—the bundle of commodities

3: Smith, Adam, and Edwin Cannan. "Of the Origin and Use of Money." The Wealth of Nations / Adam Smith ; Introduction by Alan B. Krueger ; Edited, with Notes and Marginal Summary, by Edwin Cannan. New York, NY: Bantam Classic, 2003. 43-46. Print.

that sustain the quantity of useful labor required in a commodity's production—determines the exchange value of that commodity. The difficulty in acquiring or selling a commodity helps determine its exchange value. Basic supply and demand charts represent these relationships.

The money commodity is not itself labor, but operates as though it were. Exchange value equals the quantity of the society's labor the commodity helps the purchaser command. All this means is that both the production and the purchasing of every good requires a sacrifice in terms of how much effort it takes to produce or purchase. Goods that take a lot of effort, like computers, cost much more than blueberries, which are far easier to produce.

The money economy's intensively calculative surface layer now comes into plain view. Meant to target the exchange value of given commodities, the price of a commodity is simply a reflection of the item's economic value. We can think of markets as determining this value in terms of a synthesis between space, time, and categories. But it would be a mistake to consider price as a purely rational calculation.

Panic and terror, joy and euphoria alike possess the ferocity to override cool calculation and to influence the behaviors of entire economies, not to mention the prices of individual commodities. Keeping their strategic vision perpetually trained on investing in the exchange value of assets, the authentic homo œconomicus will undoubtedly become wealthy, at least in money.

The exchange values of commodities reflected in their prices fluctuate by the second. Markets rapidly price in all up-to-the-minute information in connection with the exchange values of particular commodities. Buyers and sellers are constantly re-evaluating the prices of stocks, currency exchange rates, fuel, groceries, and so on on the basis of real time information connected with supply and demand. But does the rationalist economic system miss aspects of society in this pricing process and, if so, how badly?

# CHAPTER TWO

*Symbol Of Value And Universal Commodity*

Human societies have always used one means of exchange or another as a placeholder for value. When one of these placeholders becomes more and more favored, it becomes valuable in and of itself. This usually happens when a network of people comes to a decision about which money its members will accept as *the* money. The requirement to pay taxes in a certain monetary medium is often what sustains demand for the particular money that those within the network will accept. The individual is simply *hurled into* a world where *one* money is *the* money on the basis of taxation. This pressing demand for the money transforms the mere *symbol of value* into the *universal commodity*.

We covered in the last chapter how the purpose of money is to function as the means of exchange. The perfect money would operate as the perfect means of exchange. Money, while a special commodity, is one commodity. Societies—oftentimes vast and complex networks of cultural relationships—tend to push their particular currency toward its ultimate limit by attempting to control it such that it might represent an absolute, fixed value for trade. The fixity of the value of paper money, as opposed to coins, has made the quantity of each bill startlingly more absolute. Cryptocurrency transactions boil this down a step further by both attending to the hundred thousandth of a decimal point. The means of verification that many of these currencies employ via the complex of nodes on the blockchain, meanwhile, take this standard of converting money even further, from a mere representative means of exchange to another level of computational security: an absolute and fixed commodity. The security of a currency is crucial to the survival of the network of those who deal in it; for those within the network, money is the universal commodity. This means that money is not a mere *lingua franca* of trade, but a pure representation and crystallization of value for the individuals within that network.

Let's take a moment to acknowledge how this has progressed. The impetus to trade forced primitive societies to use commodities other than precious metals as a means of exchange. The English word pecuniary, which derives from the Latin term for money, *pecunia*, bears the mark of this origin. The Latin *pecunia* developed out of the word *pecus*, which means cattle or sheep. Livestock, agriculture, and even weapons functioned regularly as common media of exchange and as measures of value.

One can easily imagine the problems that would arise in determining the precise exchange value of a goat or a cow, or in determining the worth of a jar filled with olive oil in terms of cows or goats. Traders not only needed to appraise the value of the means of exchange, but also needed to find a person willing to trade for those means. Gold and silver, which could operate more smoothly as symbols of value, naturally followed close behind such vague—and thus vexatious—pecuniary media as livestock. As we have seen, paper and digital money as monetary technologies have the potential to advance the level of exactitude and security of a currency well beyond the capacities even of precious metals.

A distinction between two perspectives of time is crucial at this juncture. We can see that the idea of money—the commodity, in itself useless, that functions as a means of exchange—has become both increasingly useless in itself and increasingly perfected as that means of exchange. We could very well make the argument that the development of money as a technology, from cows to coins to currencies, is the result of 'thousands of years of human evolution'. But it is crucial not to limit our view of time to elementary school arithmetic. Arithmetic time watches the clock tick and tock from one moment to the next. In addition to the moment-by-moment progression of time, there is another aspect of the temporal evolutionary process. Time also progresses in terms of the unification of abstract concepts into a particular form. Cultures express the idea of money as the perfect means of exchange by inventing new and more perfected technologies. We have seen that economic networks continuously attempt to solve problems that ensure that their currency is closer and closer to substantial and absolute. That is, people try to and in some respects actually accomplish the impossible of making a pure idea a tangible item in reality. Conceptual (what we will later call 'alethic') time pushes the idea of money, which is the understanding that we need a simple way to trade, closer and closer to an absolute, abstract, and perfected commodity that operates solely as a means of exchange. The entire enterprise is founded on the assumption that a single, perfected means of exchange, capable of holding the whole array of commodities within the sphere of the human equal to some amount of itself, is possible.

Societies nevertheless attempt to push money as an idea to a perfection that is both useful and damaging. Adam Smith notes that gold functioned as the universal commodity for a time because of its relative constancy in supply. But precious metals eventually proved far from constant enough to maintain this crucial space in the economic system, both because the discovery of gold mines causes extreme price fluctuations and because the metals themselves burden traders with the difficult process of verifying quantity and authenticity. Paper money, which addresses these fundamental problems, also poses new questions. The substitution of non-precious or less-precious coins and inked paper both facilitates easy measurement and serves to fix—at least to an extent—the exchange value that the money commodity symbolizes.

We cannot understate the prevalent tendency to extend the money as a pure and absolute mathematical form—something that can be quantified, calculated, and understood—into tangible objects that at every turn resist their being reduced into numbers. The disposition toward money changes at the moment that society purports to actualize its money as the universal, constant symbol of value. But what does this mean for the individual? We've seen that money, as an idea, is this notion of a tool perfected for purposes of easy and secure exchange. At the same time, the notion of perfect money is an abstraction that can never meet with an actual currency, because a single currency simply cannot account for every aspect of value. In viewing units of labor in terms of economic quantities, we necessarily obscure different forms of value of those human entities that we naturally tend to reduce to dollar amounts. This obfuscation can certainly affect the 'bottom line'. So, what does it mean to arrive in a world of which money is a part? This is a complex question, but let's explore.

We have already made the explicit statement that, while we can speak about ideas in the abstract, real world objects *always* occur in a context. In order to understand the meaning of money as the means of exchange, measure of value, and universal commodity, we have to understand the contexts in which people find themselves. As a result, we have to discuss the principle of *the division of labor*.

Again, the classical perspective on the division of labor is the simple observation that the individual cannot supply all of their wants with the product of their own labor. Our cobbler from before can't eat shoes, so he will trade the extra shoes he produces for the other resources he needs to survive. This general truth is what makes the invention of some means of exchange necessary, because there has to be a way around having to estimate, for example, how many pairs of shoes are worth how many jars of olive oil. When we have money, we look to money to mediate such incongruous transactions. Money functions as that means of exchange. Taken to an extreme, the thought behind the division of labor is that productivity and prosperity infinitely increase as tasks are increasingly divided. Smith gives us the example of an assembly line in a factory that produces pins. Each station on the assembly line has a highly specific function. The worker only performs the task relevant to the station to which they are assigned. The thought is that having the worker at a given station, say, tap the head of each pin with a hammer at a 45° angle leads to lower production costs and *more pins*. More pins at a lower cost of production means *more profit* for the firm. This profit, the purpose of the business entity, can either be paid out in dividends or reinvested into finding ways to sell more pins at a lower production cost.

The individual who arrives in a world that prizes specialized labor is taught to target a way of life spent at a specific station on a specific assembly line. This means that the classical notion of division of labor encourages people to transfer much of their human feeling, emotion, and passion into becoming purchasable commodities. Money as the means of exchange and measure of value is not only given the power to determine the economic value of a person, but to actually force that person into a narrow range of possibilities and to buy a large part of that person's time. This universality of money compels those without money to find a way to put themselves up for sale in order to be sold.

This emotional topic can quickly devolve into folded arms and resentment, but there is little cause for alarm. This simply means that members of a society pay other members to help them toward prosperity. The universality of money guarantees its necessity. The economic system simply compels the person to find a legal and useful way to serve others.

As Marx points out, *Pecunia non olet.*[4] This literally translates as 'Money does not emit an odor'. But it simply means that money never betrays the origin—vile or high-minded—of how it was acquired. Moral standards that fall outside the realm of social or actual law do little to determine the usefulness of an activity. Because money is the universal commodity, *how* a person generates it matters very little. On this view, it would seem that the most important thing is *to find a legal way to sell your labor to others*. But legal and even social standards rely on a system of imperfect knowledge. A society that neglects to hold its members accountable for the health of that society within the spaces that the law cannot cover risks limiting its vision to a value system based largely on immediate profit.

To wrap things up, the individual gains a share of the universal commodity by offering some service to other members of society. The complexities of living out a human existence make this mutual support an absolute necessity. Because mutual support is an absolute necessity, there must be an easy way for people to exchange whatever they produce. This easy means of exchange is the particular form of money that the society 'elects'. The form of money accepted everywhere is the commodity

4: Marx, Karl, Friedrich Engels, and David Fernbach. "Money, or the Circulation of Commodities." Capital: A Critique of Political Economy. Ed. Ernest Mandel. Trans. Ben Fowkes. London: Penguin in Association with New Left Review, 1990. 267. Print.

into which all other commodities, even labor, sometimes even abstract notions like romance or friendship, can be indirectly or directly exchanged. Possession of the universal commodity entitles the possessor to a claim upon that society's goods and resources. In a utopia, the amount of money in a person's possession would correspond to the usefulness of that person to their societal network. However, money obtained legally functions as this universal claim on the goods and resources of a society, no matter the swamp or cloud from which it has been extracted.

Once we can grasp and resonate with the deeper truths about what money is and its power as a means of exchange, measure of value, and universal commodity, it becomes easier to clear our minds of the pseudo-morality that blocks us from achieving our financial goals. Making money becomes extraordinarily simple and easy. But there is of course a conflict between the possibility of making easy money and performing business activities that contribute to the health of the society on which the existence of the money depends. Moreover, it is not always clear what contributes to the health of the society and what harms it. As we have already seen, context is crucial. We will further explore these ideas in the next chapter.

# CHAPTER THREE

## *Process, Capital, And Credit*

Earlier, we alluded to the temporal aspect of money. Let's again explore this soft distinction between two aspects of time: arithmetic and alethic. We said earlier that arithmetic time simply means the passage of moments from one to the next, which roughly corresponds to addition in mathematics. Money in light of arithmetic time points us to process, capital, and credit. Alethic time is related to arithmetic time, but involves the way the individual uncovers the world by making sense of it through language and concepts. Money in terms of alethic time points us to the eventual disclosure of what money means in the life of the human being. This chapter will analyze money in light of both aspects of time, *arithmetic* and *alethic*, two intertwined elements of time itself.

We can work out money in terms of time first by analyzing money as a social process, then by recapitulating the classical views of money as capital and credit. Let's start with an example. That I possess money here now in the form of a dollar bill on my desk does little to show us what money actually is. The socioeconomic context that gives rise to money opens when we ask two simple questions: where does the money come from? And then: where is the money going? The basic intellectual error we so often make construes money, not to mention the human being, as a fixed object in space at a fixed moment in time, rather than a participant in dynamic societal processes. This arises not out of some moral defect, but out of the nature of the human imagination itself, which naturally tends to impose definite and static characteristics onto dynamic and indeterminate entities. We see this natural tendency with Kant's transcendental apperceiver, which necessarily quantifies any quantifiable aspect of its environment. But thinking that mathematics is the only tool for coming to grips with human possibility places the individual at risk of elevating economic security, in the form of a certain amount of money, to a sort of spiritual oasis in the desert of human suffering. People trade themselves, their present moment, for a financial 'someday' that would not offer them the life they desire even if they overcame the improbability of attaining it.

Money as a process must be viewed in light of the dynamic exchanges of goods and services between members of society. We can view this process roughly in terms of mathematics or language. While mathematics helps us understand and quantify commodities in economic terms, language helps us tackle what has either yet to be quantified, or that which cannot be. Knowledge of these dual aspects of time serves as no guarantee that an individual will thwart all financial difficulty—the insignificance of individual effort and greatness against the total tide of cosmos, world, and human history is the essence of tragedy. Karatani's reading of Kant and Marx informs us about the danger of this fundamental conflation between mathematics and language.

The individual *cannot help* but view money as an infinitely expanding entity, because of the correlation between money and the arithmetic progression of time that we will soon explore. However, the perspective of money, of time, and of the world that thoughtlessly reduces *all entities* to economic quantities fundamentally misses the very point of human existence. The alethic dimension of time that analyzes the world through thought and language is the tool that can free us from obscuring the deeper aspects of truth from our vision. Instead of limiting the goal to making a better profit, the goal can expand into making a better world. But there is little incentive to focus on creating a better world, because money has so much power to allow individuals to purchase what cannot be quantified. Aeschylus makes it clear through the mouth of Prometheus that even optimal skill cannot outpace fate and necessity. But Freud astutely points us to making an effort toward mutual love and care as the only reasonable course of action.

We have seen that two separate but related elements comprise money as a process. Let's now turn to money as capital. In a purely arithmetic sense, capital signifies the future value of money. This is why popular authors like Robert Kiyosaki insist that the reader put their money to work for them by buying assets. The classic example of this is the bank's service of loaning money now in exchange for receiving that money back plus interest. If the dollar bill on my desk has been loaned out at interest, the dollar can no longer represent a dollar, but must point to a longer-term flow of capital *back* to the people who loaned it. Perhaps I must pay the creditor $1.06 in a month's time. Money seen as the universal commodity can lead some to shift the reason why they spend their money. When money becomes capital, the individual no longer exchanges money for commodities to be used, but employs their money to the end of making more money. Money that exists purely for the sake of making more money is what the term *capital* means. All sorts of financial problems can arise when the individual fails to make healthy distinctions between the money that exists here and now and the other kind.

Alethic time works on another level of being, and this shift in the essence of being translates money into an entity altogether separate from the pure quantitative approach of arithmetic time. The term *alethic* derives from the Greek ἀλήθεια (alētheia), which is poorly translated as 'truth'. Martin Heidegger offers another possibility with the German *Erschlossenheit*, usually rendered in English as 'disclosure'. This 'disclosure' involves the process of making sense of phenomena in a given range of understanding. All meaningful phenomena happen within the contextual space of how the individual understands the 'world'. Experiential phenomena draw into play the deep conceptual foundations of human sense-making and populate the world and life of the individual. Time in the alethic sense is the processual uncovering of 'what' the individual already knows itself to be. It less concerns the progressive ticking up or down of a financial quantity than it does the relationship the individual assumes to that dynamic quantity. Rather than subordinating oneself to the process of money as capital, the aspect of alethic time allows the individual to subordinate money as capital merely to serve a greater purpose for itself.

We have said that money is not an object, but a process. This simple perception throws the notion of money as a quantity into chaos, because, even as a quantity, it is never fixed. Strict fundamental analysis in investing transposes a projected future capital appreciation onto current accounting data. The alethic process of capital would operate perhaps more fundamentally to human existence, because it would allow for a direct perspective of social responsibility instead of purely financial responsibility. Of course, both are crucial. But with the alethic conception in mind, investment and business activity gains a level of integrity that pure economic analysis cannot provide. The Greek historian Herodotus offers a clean contrast between arithmetic thinking and alethic thinking.

In his notorious *Histories*, the Greek historiographer Herodotus tells us about the visit of Solon, mythical lawgiver of Athens, to the Lydian Empire.[5] Croesus, the king of Lydia, had accumulated vast stores of wealth and had built a dreamy palace for himself. Solon, meanwhile, after having given the Athenians their laws, had left Athens for 10 years so as not to be coerced into repealing them. During this decade-long hiatus, Solon travelled both to Egypt and to Sardis, the capital of then-flourishing Lydia in what is now Turkey. Having heard of Solon's wisdom and travels, Croesus had his attendants give Solon a tour of the palace and its vast material treasures. Rather sure of the answer to the question, Croesus says: Solon, I've heard so much about your wisdom and your travels—I'd like to know: who's the most fortunate man you've ever met? And Solon, lawgiver of Athens, shocks Croesus by saying: Great King, without a doubt, the most fortunate man I've ever met is Tellus the Athenian. Croesus cannot understand how Solon could have seen the immense wealth and fortune of his kingdom and still have considered Tellus, an everyday Athenian citizen, as the

5: Hdt. 1.130-2.

most fortunate man he had ever met. Croesus says: But why?! How in the world is it Tellus? Solon replies: Well, he was from a flourishing city and had good children. All his children had grandchildren, all of whom survived. He was financially prosperous and died fighting the Athenian enemy. The Athenians paid for his burial and honored him at his death.

Croesus stands there befuddled. The conversation continues as Solon describes to Croesus a view essential to Greek wisdom: that you can't judge a man until he has completed his entire life. All of Croesus's wealth does not entail that either he or his children and people will thrive like Tellus's people did. Herodotus brings the myth to an end by describing how Cyrus the Great of Persia eventually overthrew Croesus and seized his meaningless wealth.

Tellus the Athenian used money to provide himself with the basic necessities of life. Croesus used his power to engender yet more money in the hope that this would make him safe. But financial security is a small aspect of safety. Money as a phenomenon of human existence is not a product of man, not a tool of man, but in some sense is man, insofar as man's being is bound to the body that requires society and commerce for upkeep. But there is a limit to what degree of wealth is prudent. Arithmetic views of money allow only for a myopic vision for existence. This zombie-like absent-mindedness threatens to reduce the entirety of human existence to the pursuit of increasing capital limitlessly from one moment to the next. There is nothing wrong with increasing capital, but doing so thoughtlessly alienates individuals from themselves. This way of seeing the world reduces the human to an entity that exists purely for the sake of adding, adding, and adding ad infinitum to a store of the particular medium of exchange. The perspective of alethic time disrupts the madness by pointing out that nothing less than the continuity of society and the person's individual life stand to be won or lost by means of self-application that is correct or incorrect on the basis of personal values. That is not to say that arithmetic money is useless, dirty, or foolish—instead, it must be considered in light of the whole. Alethic time is the lever that challenges the natural tendency of the human intellect to imagine all the entities in its world in relation to their economic quantity, even in the event that the perspective that money is purely meant to be increased takes such a hold that it obscures an individual's vision.

While the term money often calls to mind a particular commodity, which commodity societies use as money stands subject to rapid and unpredictable change. This is why money as a universal concept has little to do with what particular commodity societies use as money. The universal concept of money refers to the medium of exchange that societies push toward a pure ideation of value. This should come as no surprise, because we have already discussed the evolution of precisely which commodities different societies have used to facilitate trade. Particular commodities like cattle, bushels of wheat, precious metals, and paper currencies all operate as conceptual placeholders. The word *money* will always conjure two separate notions: one, the money phenomenon as an idea, which I have hitherto referred to as the pure idea or the universal concept of money, and the other, the particular moneys that societies use—US Dollars or Euros, for instance. But another aspect of the process of money involves the anxious desire to pretend that a particular instantiation of the money commodity— the US Dollar, for example—actually is the universal concept.

The corporate model that flourishes in capitalism often resembles a biomimetic blend between orgasm, people pleasing, and homicide. The successful manipulation of the shareholder capital in arithmetic terms threatens to become an object of fanatical worship—shadowy investors become ominous deities worthy of superstitious reverence. Shareholder oversight, which holds firms accountable to rigorous growth targets, produces a grueling work environment that often only supports the more fundamental forms of healthy society informally and coincidentally. The emphasis is on increasing the quantity of the raw facts of material existence; this myopic vision leaves space for little recognition of the more fundamental alethic qualities of the human being. A vision that accounts for the whole human being and society in the long run could make production much more efficient, but necessity constrains business people to get to cash immediately. There is no exit from the unbridled and seemingly dominant necessity to win the perpetual increase of shareholder profits. But businesses that make it their entire basis to serve their shareholders immediately while harming the society at large are parasitic to the very social processes that give them life. Arithmetic time has to be tempered by the holistic view of society and individual. Plain and simple, profit can never actually be the bottom line, only an aspect of it.

The problem is deeper than economics. The error arises from the thought that a limited aim, even that of having a prosperous society or state, can serve as an all-encompassing guide to any and every human action. Any dedication to a shortsighted life-purpose that does not prize the maximized prosperity of the individual potentially renders that prosperity impossible. Thus, it cannot be left to *any system* of mathematics, logic, or language to guarantee that prosperity, but is a continuous struggle that occurs on an individual basis in response to the boring dynamics of coercive power. The monetary system is yet another system that the individual must resolve to take ownership of. While the necessity of caring for one's physical body obviates any possibility for an incorporeal freedom, the only proper choice is to take hold of the purest of those possibilities for the sake of oneself. This alethic perspective of capital disrupts the tyranny of arithmetic capital. In any case, human beings cannot escape that they are on some level the ones who make decisive responses to their own environments. The determination to make profit at any expense requires a human mind to make such a determination.

It is far from the case that all employment or business activity is the new inferno. Providing other members of society with services remains the only reliable way to take ownership of a portion of the money commodity—the vital essence of society—for oneself. I use such colorful language to give light to the longing for immortality that drives the absurd madness to subordinate one's decision-making faculties *in toto* to capital increase. The existential *there* must be sought outside of arithmetic capital generation, even if it is attained in regard to arithmetic capital, because the capital itself cannot ever contain the value the mind invests in it. If the arithmetic growth of capital is a person's ultimate purpose, the mind is what determines it to be so. The decision to focus on generating profit is in itself neither right nor wrong. We have seen how powerful and beautiful it is to possess money in order to exchange money for the necessaries of life. But it is circumstance, not the joy of spending money, that dictates whether or not aiming at profit is a valid decision.

Nigel Dodd observes that Marx had a boring perspective on capital. Marx's project comes off as quasi-sarcastic.[6] Marx thought that money represents the "economic, social, and moral value [of a society]." This can't be a serious statement, but is a poetic one, written by a persona-donning creative. Of course *nobody* insofar as they are human can possibly be so asinine and petty as to allow money to represent moral value, regardless of how serious an effort so many make to earn such titles. A human being would have to be so deranged, dissociated, and deformed in their humanity to use money as the capital that Marx describes that we could no longer reasonably call such a person 'human'. There is always a higher order of the ultimate purpose involved in spending, earning, and value placement. But perhaps Marx has a point, because not all life decisions are—or even can be—well informed. Moralizing about the limitations of human vision does less to solve the grotesque problems it creates than it does to produce long-lasting resentments and obstacles to playing well with others. Prosperity need not be a zero-sum game.

But Marx is far from a deliberate ass. Money does become capital when the local purpose of spending it changes.[7] Money as capital designates the shift in what

6: Dodd, Nigel, and Nigel Dodd. "Chapter 2: Capital." The social life of money. Princeton, NJ: Princeton U Press, 2014. 104. Print.

7: Marx, Karl, Friedrich Engels, and David Fernbach. "Money, or the Circulation of Commodities." Capital: A Critique of Political Economy. Ed. Ernest Mandel. Trans. Ben Fowkes. London: Penguin in Association with the person *thinks money is*, even if the individual's thinking distorts the locus wherein that thinking occurs. When money is seen as capital, the intention of spending the money is always in order to make more money. This can be carried to the extreme of thinking that the purpose of *human life as such* is to use money as capital. Investment is the simplest and most obvious example. Fundamental analysis involves the location of underpriced assets.

Investors give money to the managers of businesses because they believe that the managers will be able to generate a percentage return on that money. But this way of spending money in order to generate more of it ruptures the capitalized money from the more fundamental uses of it, such as purchasing food or clothing. The fanaticism to earn money in order to spend it in chaos can likewise produce ruptures in the real sense of satisfaction that making positive contributions to history, society, and one's own personal relationships can offer. These pleasures, while in no way guaranteed, seem to be the only veritable source of inspiration and meaning.

Many popular books on finance are slyly philosophical. In *Rich Dad, Poor Dad*, Robert Kiyosaki gives his reader the simplest advice imaginable: *buy assets*. The purchase of or investment in an asset is, as Kiyosaki continually reminds us, *making money work for you*. Warren Buffett is credited with saying: If you don't

New Left Review, 1990. 267. Print.

find a way to make money while you sleep, you will work until you die. Nothing else is meant by the notion of money as capital: the person who spends money on food and clothing becomes the investor who spends money for the sake of earning a return on that expenditure. For Marx, this shift in how society uses money—from buying commodities for personal consumption to investing money in order to make more money—constitutes the metamorphosis of money into capital.

But even those who apply money as capital cannot fully sever themselves from the more fundamental reason that they would spend money as capital to begin with. That things will go awry when money becomes capital does not constitute the only possibility for its application. Money as capital is simply a technology that people can choose to ignore, hate, or use for their own benefit.

Before we move onto the technical aspects of money as credit, we must take a clue from our concept of alethic time. Marx unveils the perspectival and relative nature of alethic money through his dialectical treatments. His basic point of view is that the 'group' of people who own the assets are able to keep them in their possession indefinitely. He thinks that there are two basic classes in a capitalist society: bourgeois and proletariat. For Marx, the bourgeois control the capital and makes access to capital impossible for the proletariat. He sees the proletariat as the sort of person who is *forced* to live *paycheck to paycheck.* This is ultimately what he means by money as credit. Money is credit for the person who pays interest on the capital. It serves merely to cancel the proletariat's debt to the bourgeois capital manager. Not having money feels much like a boot in the ass that strongly encourages a person into exploiting their own labor in order to generate a share of the essence of society. On the Marxist view, one 'class' has greater access to prosperity than another 'class'.

Marx seems to have believed that one social class oppresses another, perpetually, by means of paying low wages for labor. If what he says is true in a fundamental sense, then the people whom the 'system' maims would have some sort of non-deductible insurance claim on the rest of society. The term social class makes it sound like there is an explicit or implicit bourgeois conspiracy to keep the heel of the boot on the neck of the so-called prole. But one wonders who is really responsible for the lifelong adherence to a victim's framework.

Attributable to Marx or not, Marxist resentments seem to do more to promote the victim mentality than to teach people how to navigate the financial system in order to get off of the hamster wheel. Change can become actual through a culture that values truth and properly identifies and calls out exploitation.

Generally speaking, the people whom the system does not benefit still want a state to step in and negotiate laws on their behalf, which will lead to a better bargain. Perhaps this can be a fruitful endeavor, but it nevertheless relies on an external source to give people what already lies in their own power to accomplish. Life and business are challenging, and not everybody wins. But why turn to *another* state solution? Marxism shows many important truths, but risks trapping its imprudent disciples within an identity of a social class that limits their possibilities for action. Kant, in his *What is Enlightenment?*, empowers the individual not to cower from or to neglect their own power. The proposal of another state solution to the problem simply remains trapped in the feedback loop that the total solution must come from outside oneself. If a person is disempowering themselves by claiming that an ominous 'upper class' is 'oppressing' them, they will benefit greatly from accepting where they actually are, deciding on self-respect, truth, and clarity, and getting to work on creating the life that they want from where they actually stand.

Victimhood as a lifestyle usually has its roots in traumatic experiences that low cost or even free mental health services and support groups can help people to resolve. This message is not meant to condone or shill for the cruel reality of human life, but to empower any person who thinks that they will be rewarded by a state apparatus for having been victimized to believe that they can enrich themselves by means of their own studies and actions. For purposes of this book, that means working to develop skills to understand money and business. An understanding of money as alethic makes it possible to use money as credit for one's own benefit.

Although I just offered a practical critique of the Marxist view of implications of money as credit, money still is credit. The capitalist system provides self-subjugating people with infinite opportunities for working paycheck to paycheck. The system will absolutely wreck a person who does not exercise caution or who thinks that the end days are nigh and that, as they swear it, the Debt Christ, redeemer of coupons, will apocalyptically break into the framework of history in order to forgive the sins of a lifelong addiction to costly bullshit. The window toward financial freedom is really quite narrow. Our notion of money as capital leads one directly to the contemplation of who has the money, what makes it grow, and who benefits from that growth. Thus, money is always *that which must be paid back*. Alethic money tells us resoundingly to place that money *into our own* accounts. But we have said little about the more technical aspects of money as credit, which point us to a discussion of the relationship between governments and global financial institutions.

The distinction between states and banks is no longer clean, as the relationships between financial institutions and national governments have become increasingly interdependent. The approach of reducing labyrinthine economic processes to logical, theorized models for understanding serves an academic and pedagogical purpose that is of less use in later portions of the book. We will keep these theories as basic as possible. It is neither national governments nor particular banks, but the money concept that has always survived the numerous crises, revolutions, and technological media that have undermined and uprooted the political ideals on which states are founded. This raises the question of what, or what sort of thing, *the state actually is* and to what extent the actual state relates to what we call it. Still, let us apply the distinction between state and bank, treating them as imaginarily separate, in order to analyze the problem of *money as credit* more soundly.

The first technical perspective of *money as credit* subordinates money to the state. This phenomenon is still in some sense extant. On this view, the state levies taxes in the form of payment it is willing to accept. And the state always levies taxes on the citizen by placing the citizen under the threat of violence. As we mentioned earlier, the necessity of paying taxes to the state creates a demand for the currency that the government or society agrees to accept. Money, then, serves to do nothing more than cancel this tax-debt—that is, money is "...the opportunity to cancel a debt."[8] The debt that money serves to cancel is classically thought of as debt to the state. But, as Mitchell-

8: Dodd, Nigel, and Nigel Dodd. "Chapter 1: Origins." The social life of money. Princeton, NJ: Princeton U Press, 2014. 104. Print.

Innes says, money is "credit and nothing but credit."[9] This simply means that the money has no use in human life outside of being a medium of exchange. In terms of credit, fiat money is like monopoly money. But a government's decision to accept a particular currency as payment for taxes qualifies *one* money as *the* money.[10] On this view, it would seem that post-Bretton Woods system uses another commodity or set of commodities to back the fiat currencies.[11] Some would argue that military might gives

---

9: Mitchell-Innes, A. "What Is Money? By A. Mitchell Innes." What Is Money? By A. Mitchell-Innes. N.p., n.d. Web. 11 Jan. 2017.

10: Wray, L. Randall. Understanding modern money: the key to full employment and price stability. Cheltenham, Glos, UK: Edward Elgar, 77. 1998. Print.

11: I have heard many people whisper in panicky, shallow breaths that money is just an idea, as though it were a terrible secret. Kant rightly says: *Concepts without intuition are blind.* Indeed, money is not simply an idea, but also an experiential object, right here, in my face, as tangible as it is intelligible. The money concept would be fanciful without some everyday, grounded notion of that which the talk is about. Money as money is the direct opposite of what those who consider it a fiction worry it may be: it's the universal manifestation of economic value for the whole society that accepts its legitimacy. Simmel shows us by his radical re-appropriation of the classical metaphysical term 'substance' that, far from our money *wanting* a connection to the concrete, much of what comprises the society *goes into* the money and what is meant by the configurations of experience that quantities of money represent. In certain respects, the money is, on the contrary, *not abstract enough*, and in fact too rigid in its ability to render a state of exception across the spectrum of social mores. Money as such is the commodity for which all others can be exchanged. As a result, the dollar is far from under duress as a result of having been taken off of the gold standard, and is perhaps more closely tied to a more actual essence. That in mind, if the keepers of the currency take too much liberty in their poetic urges, like Susan Strange describes in *Casino Capitalism*, then there is again reason to discuss the set of problems that have become cliché since the 2007-8 Financial Crisis. If the task is to devise a ranking of aspects of money according to net harm done, the capacity of excess money to suspend any

the state—that is, whoever controls the political process—the right to declare what currency the state will accept in taxation. As this is a rarefied conceptual perspective, it is all the more important to think broadly insofar as what the state is and what its boundaries are. The classical political language of statehood likely does not meet the challenge of describing the web of international relationships and shifting alliances and connections that influence economic dimensions. As related to the ostensible state, money as credit serves to cancel the individual's debt to its government.

Mitchell-Innes, whom we quoted earlier, argued that the state does not have the power to declare what currency will hold value. This leads us to the second perspective on money as credit, which views money in light of the major financial and political institutions, to which all loans must eventually be repaid. It is in fact banks that create money by means of accepting deposits and loaning them out at interest. In exchange for some money, they receive *more* money *in the future*. The government in this case merely acts as a loan-guarantor on behalf of its citizens (for example, the Emergency Economic Stabilization Act of 2008: the US Government bailed out major financial institutions who had purchased debts with variable interest rates that debtors could no longer repay). The creditors extend credit to debtors at the principal * 1 +

---

form of value except for that of immediate transaction seems a far more damaging phenomenon.

the interest rate. The debtor must repay the *future* value of the money loaned—and all money emanates from this money-creation schema. In handing out loans at interest, capital is able, as Marx put it, to "lay golden eggs".[12] What enraged the Aristotelian Marx was that banks should have the power to do this at all—the Marxist views labor as the productive force, not capital. On this view, the usurious banks swipe unearned value from those to whom they loan the money at interest. Whether the state or global financial institutions finally exact the punishments on the debtor for failing to meet debt obligations, debt is doubtless a four-letter word.

The nature of being compelled to borrow for the sake of education, housing, or basic nutrition forces individuals to offer an increasingly large cut of their future labor for the sake of achieving their simple personal goals. But, in general, the American government understands that its own wellbeing relies on the health of its citizens. While Marx thinks that capital eventually congeals around a certain class of people who control it and force others into a generationally paycheck-by-paycheck way of life, student loans properly applied are a means to pay for an education with a loan at low interest. While nature proves itself empty and merciless, the masked villain is certainly not other people in general, as participation in a healthy

12: Marx, Karl, Ben Fowkes, and David Fernbach. Capital: a critique of political economy. London: Penguin in association with New Left Review, 1981. 255. Print.

society is actually the only hope for securing personal fulfillment. Money as credit is thoroughly paradoxical: while the material of which it is made is less useful than kindling for a fire, fiat money is simultaneously the economic cornerstone of the society in which it has value.

In terms of exchange rates and the value of currency, the interest rate determines the value of money. Thus, the interest rate serves as an indicator of government mediation—an increase in interest rates favors large financial institutions, while a decrease favors the producers and consumers. The federal interest rate, then, can be seen as a sort of tug-of-war between lenders and borrowers. On this view, any money loaned is credit, in that the creditor holds the debtor liable for repayment. Moreover, only large financial institutions create money by this process of loaning at interest.

This division between the government, banks, and we, the people, is of course a simplistic view. The large financial institutions do much more than loan out money. Moreover, those who comprise the banking system often constitute the very body of producers and consumers to whom it loans money in the form of mortgages and student loans. Similarly, certain modes of production entail loans of a kind, when the product cannot be immediately consumed. On the whole, however, money viewed as credit sees money as the opportunity to cancel out a liability, either to the government or to the lender.

Hyman Minsky, whom we will meet in the next chapter, observed that the financial system itself promotes the very sort of money-managerial, speculative capitalism that generates the inevitable rupture between the value of labor beneficial to society and the value of credit money, which has no necessary relationship to any form of human productivity. Financial actors are increasingly able to securitize and package more and more aspects of everyday reality. Credit money is the phenomenon of the absolute disconnection between the hard value produced by human labor and the printed money that has its value in the lie that it can attain the unattainable. That is, credit money tells us that it can reduce every object in the space of economics to a mathematical quantity.

Moreover, credit money wants us to believe that everything to which an economic value can be ascribed is actually an asset. This allows us to dick around with far more money than we actually have. One classic style of dicking around with money is the Ponzi Scheme. Credit money not only allows an economy the unlimited capacity to extract money from valueless assets, but more importantly makes it possible for the money that comes from the hard labor that benefits the continuity of a society to be held precisely equal to money invented by using language to pump up the 'value' of a worthless asset. The pure idiocy that holds equal the worthless money and the necessary arises directly from what necessarily *has to happen*, if any currency is to fulfill its most basic function of making trade between diverse constituents as simple as possible. What boggles the mind is not that credit money exists, for it must. Instead, there are two important questions: first, how is it possible that a lack of money terrorizes so many people, when money itself is a pure fiction that has no necessary connection whatsoever to the genuine value that ensures the health and continuity of a society? Second, whose job is it to predict precisely what economic quantity a given commodity, such as the labor of a person, is worth?

# CHAPTER FOUR

## *Ponzi Finance And Anonymity*

We have covered quite a bit of ground since the beginning of this text. What's important to see is that fiat money is a double-edged invention that arises out of necessity. While it beautifully solves numerous fundamental problems—for it fosters efficient trade, precise measurements, and stability in the monetary supply—it makes possible two more obstacles that relate to the way that we as a society elect to think of time. The purpose of money in terms of arithmetic time, which naturally understands money as an entity that expands infinitely as time progresses, is purely to achieve that infinite expansion. In a recession or depression, this tendency gets turned upside down.

The human being tends to prophesy ominously that 'the economy may never recover'. Economic recovery, of course, is defined as the achievement of the fetish of infinite growth. But the purpose of money through the lens of alethic time takes into account a wider array of phenomena than simply the endless augmentation of one's holdings in a particular currency. Consumers decide between useful and useless products. Capitalism as a forceful impetus to innovate in ways that members of society can immediately recognize calls for a 'no-nonsense' approach to business. At the same time, we have seen that nonsense is necessarily a partial basis for all commodities that are to serve as money. This conscripts the members of society to focus solely on activities that generate money *right away*.

The urgent and immediate need of money means that the money itself, which reduces labor to a quantity of itself that is fundamentally worthless *without* the human being, has intruded further and further into the alethic spaces. That is to say, the act of stockpiling an abstract quantity of a form of money has become a surrogate for a meaningful life. Capitalism, a dumb technological standard that forces arithmetic economic growth, simply lacks the fine-grained sensitivity to circumstance that a holistic perspective of human prosperity requires. This system measures how well it adds to itself, not how well it is.

Let's turn now to the work of Hyman Minksy. The sketch provided in the previous chapters discloses the temporal nature of money, which always points us toward a *future* that we understand in terms of the *past*.

Money strangely summons people from where they will be going. This means that money supposedly increases or decreases with each tick and tock in a perfect and logical accordance with the moments that immediately preceded the present one.

Minksy sees the monetary system as a "pyramid of interbank liabilities." Dodd writes, "According to Minsky, trouble always starts for Ponzi finance as inflation builds and the authorities try to exorcise it through monetary restraint. Rising interest rates lead to rising debt costs, whereupon 'the net worth of previous Ponzi units will quickly evaporate.'"[13]

The finitude and fragile essence of the human body and mind makes it inevitable that individuals, businesses, and entire societies will make bogus speculative investments of labor or capital. The collapse of these bogus units is as natural as death or even defecation. What predates the bubble is a rash and romantic mood of radical, romantic optimism that, as Dodd characterizes it, "nothing will change in the near future." Ponzi units are those that simply make terrible bets that worthless assets will eventually appreciate.

But we can see that the natural fetishism of the human understanding, which thinks of money as getting infinitely bigger, makes speculative investing a hallmark of the free markets. This is the same element that drives risky innovations—the personal computer, for instance—that, when successful, vastly benefit society.

13: Dodd, Nigel, and Nigel Dodd. "Chapter 3: Debt." The social life of money. Princeton, NJ: Princeton U Press, 2014. 119. Print.

When we speak of speculative investing, we're not simply speaking of hedge fund managers. A student who takes out massive student loans for the sake of getting a private, liberal arts education, for example, is as much a speculator as a wobbly Wall Street don.

It should now be clear that all economic activity as a bet on a future value is at least partially speculative. The most precise, sophisticated, and profitable trading and investment strategies place supreme emphasis on risk management precautions that protect capital. Some risk management systems—both in investment and labor—are much more wholesome than others. Even Kant's transcendental apperceiver is no match for the unpredictability of price action. Now, we could certainly do the boring thing and offer prophecies about exactly when the next credit collapse will occur. We could talk about student loans, credit cards, and increases in interest rates. This all would serve little purpose, because nobody would believe it anyway. It should by now be resoundingly true that credit bubbles are a hallmark of free enterprise. But the bank runs, panic attacks, and covert cannibalism that happen during economic downturns occur purely out of a scarcity-minded and childish paranoia.

Dodd refers to variations of the doomsday style of thinking as *austerity myths*. These foolish mythologies take particularly vicious hold during economic contractions. The thought arises from the same foolish rigidity that views money as a pure arithmetic function. Having seen the economy take a major or even minor dip, panic slowly sets in, and people begin to make severe spending cuts. But these long-term adherences to the sort of scarcity-mindedness that good psychotherapy can heal nearly always ignore the broader, alethic perspective that shows how seriously such short-sighted, arithmetic thinking damages the very bottom line that it is instituted to protect.

In abstracting the human being from the entire context of its existence and into an economic quantity, it's easy for employers and members of society at large to justify brutal decisions by telling themselves: *This is a business.* Of course, middle management has the boot to the back of their necks just the same. But this practice of creating fiat money out of dubious assets and then, when the bubble pops, reducing whoever is caught off guard to the level of excrement by firing them at the worst possible moment, ignores the severe consequences of decontextualizing and therefore dehumanizing the human being whose angst remains unimportant, ignored, and impolite to express.

A credit crisis is a fun game, a sort of social value hot potato. You don't want to get caught having made a speculative investment in, say, a college education, nor do you want to wind up as an employee with an inefficient company, or you could soon find yourself in a wet sleeping bag on a sidewalk in the Haight. During a credit collapse, employers ultimately must determine who has immediate arithmetic value and who doesn't. Of course, the shortsightedness that ignores the social costs of sending a person into the network of absurdly inefficient government bureaucracies causes an immense degree of suffering that the entire society eventually bears. These people who suffer are not simply nameless 'employees', but are mothers, fathers, sons, brothers, sisters, and daughters. The definition of anonymity in our sense is being absolutely decontextualized by means of having been reduced to an economic quantity.

Capitalistic anonymity is a basic attitude of irresponsibility for oneself in terms of a relationship to others. Having already absolutely dehumanized oneself into the form of an economic quantity that only has value in an intellectual 'someday', all that remains to offer others is identical treatment. As soon as a person can be swapped for a more viable asset, the arithmetic value system makes this replacement a necessity. It has no capacity to identify the long-term repercussions that placing serious strain on those with whom the decontextualized individual comes into contact will have on society.

It's not wise either to inveigh against service to others or even against trading labor for money. Reducing oneself to the function of a tool, which is compensated in proportion to its usefulness, is the battle-axe of many legendary figures within history. But it is strange to declare that every person, despite their various aspects, ought to be directly translatable into a currency with which their lives as a whole are largely incommensurable. It would be much wiser to ensure that, during the inevitable credit crises inherent in capitalism, some sort of care system, and not one solely reliant on inefficient government bureaucracies, would make sure that there is no financial carnage for any one person, in order that entire families or communities are not affected. Again, blockchain technology offers an intriguing possibility for the purpose of creating a pure and efficient means to identify *individuals*, not just global financial institutions, who are in desperate need of cash, and to get them immediate access to resources. As of now, it seems that the current system has accidentally taken literally the advice of Jonathan Swift in *Modest Proposal*. The proposition of setting up a sort of safety net that would spring into action during a credit crisis is as much a moral imperative as it is a pragmatic one.

We may now open a direct discussion of the real impact of the damages of placing arithmetic time ahead of alethic time. The arithmetic perspective desperately clings to a fantasy of an ever-expanding, financial 'bottom-line'. The alethic perspective, however, better stresses the connectivity between strangers and those within one's 'own' network. While unable to solve such difficult problems, a person who is not poor may at least understand the long-term, karmic consequences of the poverty of others as an event that will inevitably affect them just as well. In the developed world, something as simple as a minor interest rate increase can have devastating consequences on the ability of borrowers to meet their payment obligations. We have seen that money as the universal commodity, because it represents the capacity to secure food and shelter, has a direct linkage with the capacities of the human body. Excessive debt makes basic self-care more difficult, as money goes to the repayment of the debt rather than nutrition, education, and healthcare. When repayment becomes increasingly difficult, that means that this debt, which had been packaged and sold as an asset, can no longer rightly be considered an asset. In addition to losing out on basic necessities, a link in the chain of interconnected liabilities simply goes offline and potentially puts the whole centralized system at risk.

Michel Foucault writes in *Discipline and Punish* about the trend in the prison system of turning the disciplinary focus away from the corporal mutilation of criminals and instead imposing norms and routines on the prisoners. He contrasts the brutal execution of Robert-François Damiens in 1757 for attempted regicide with a disciplinary method that uses a regimen and schedule to reform the behaviors of the incarcerated, two approaches only separated by a century. The financial system, on the other hand, has *increasingly* laid claim to, securitized, and packaged into a financial quantity the bare biological fact of human life. State nationalism has historically proven powerless to prevent the bad infinity of this unlimited securitization from taking place. The free-market poetics of the financial system continuously increases its claim on the naked fact of the human body. In such a system, money becomes a method of paying interest on the loan of one's own biotic existence. As the autonomy over one's own body becomes more and more a political ideal, financial institutions have become less and less regulated in their capacity to create credit out of the raw reality of human corpses.

The economic cost of the 2008 credit collapse is still being tallied. The New York Times estimates it to be a loss of somewhere in the $50,000 - $150,000 range for the lifetime income expectations of working adults.[14] Other effects are more difficult to measure. As Minksy noted, the question is not *if* another crisis will arise, but *when*, because the financial system itself thrives on the mode of speculative finance that creates credit panics.

The diseconomies of scale in the American political and economic structure produce an atmosphere of social irresponsibility for oneself in relation to other people.

---

14: Porter, E. (2014, January 21). Recession's True Cost Is Still Being Tallied. Retrieved March 22, 2017, from: https://www.nytimes.com/2014/01/22/business/economy/the-cost-of-the-financial-crisis-is-still-being-tallied.html?_r=0

Psychology in some way refers to this as 'the bystander effect'. In certain sectors of the business world, nearly anything goes. *If I don't do it, someone else will* is the slogan of many successful entrepreneurs and businesses, at least in respect to *some* aspect of their business activity. While the American capitalist system starves for greater social accountability—more people speaking up more often— the brilliance of the capitalist system is the possibility for individuals to decide on their own needs and meet them. In a vestige of human sacrifice, certain corners of the press tap into this primal urge to hold someone responsible by stringing up clueless public figures as scapegoats accountable for the whole of society's problems. This approach to communication has created a hostile political climate in which it seems that such deep dissatisfaction and difference can only be expressed in the reeking form of physical violence. The basis of this is a political form of anonymity and decontextualization that happens due to the same commitment to increasing capital arithmetically at the expense of the alethic possibilities for actually solving problems. The decontextualized and sociopathic way of life in the realm of economics and relationships ultimately claims for itself no responsibility for the effects of its profiteering on the rest of society.

While the problem of Ponzi finance is inherent in the credit system, the issue of anonymity has its roots in a form of self-negation that amounts to a prolonged form of social suicide. In *The Sickness Unto Death*, Kierkegaard very lucidly explains the problem of abstracting oneself into an infinity as a form of *despair*, which is *the desire to be rid of oneself.* Despair is the emotional state of the self that turns against itself. Despair in terms of money is a form of self-loathing compounded with fear. The person, who cannot un-person their personhood, desperately wants to be someone else—that is, *to die*—except they dread the prospect of actually crossing over into the undiscovered country. Rather than self-acceptance, a form of pathological thinking arises: the thought is that a certain amount of money or social status will suffice to control the perpetually jangling alarm of trauma and self-hatred. Because life has seemingly lost all tangible value for such a person, nothing can stop them beyond a form of social restraint. We know that credit crises are inherent features of capitalist markets. When immediate profit is the *modus operandi* for capitalist businesses, it is not only wise for governments to bailout global financial institutions, but also individual investors, whose speculative housing purchases sank them into the total loss of bankruptcy through a fault of their own that was no less reprehensible than that of the institutions who lent and then packaged and sold the debt in the first place.

# CONCLUSION

We've just taken a grand tour through basic social topography of the landscape of monetary theory. It should by now be clear that money cannot be considered a definite and fixed object, but is instead two interrelated things: both an abstract idea that constitutes a perfect way of making economic transactions and a particular technology that purports to serve this purpose. We have seen that paper money as a technology beautifully solves numerous problems. At the same time, credit money extracted from assets of dubious economic value involves the looming potential that some of the 'money' will become completely dislocated from the genuine productivity that it is supposed to represent. These credit bubbles, as Minsky reminds us, are a normal part of the everyday functioning of a capitalist economy. It is less strange that these cycles exist than that what we know will necessarily happen because of the system's structure still surprises us and results in such terrible harms.

It's true that we don't know when the next credit collapse will happen. The possibility of another economic crisis has led to a brand of financial messianism, in which financial analysts and thinkers soothsay a coming series of end days that is always just around the corner. While there is always a market for such entertainment, neither this apocalyptic thinking nor the neglect of the inherent structural defects of credit money can account for a solution to the problem. By applying the power of Minksy-ite analysis, we can actually separate paroxysmal emotional reactions from the banal routine of the flow of capital away from assets revealed to be risky. This means that we can actually anticipate what before seemed like severe credit collapses without hallucinatory paranoia. Historically, these are minor corrections.

Though the rich will suffer greatly as well, the lower and middle classes have more reason for alarm. People who are arbitrarily determined not to be valuable to society on the grounds of their productivity—or lack thereof—in terms of arithmetic capital face top down impositions of austerity. After 2008, it should be clear enough that forcing austerity onto the 'lower classes' worsens or itself causes financial crises, because financial institutions themselves have balance sheets that depend on the en masse debts of the poor.

The system currently allows those who cannot pay to be drawn into decontextualized abstractions, ignoring the hard economic value at risk by allowing entire families to lapse into financial oblivion. The extreme waste and inefficiency inherent in capitalistic business should reveal that there are plenty of resources to go around, even in a vicious economic downturn. Corporate entities, which rely on the health of the consumers for their own well being, likely have a greater capacity to respond to economic crises than inefficient government bureaucracies. This was the case during Hurricane Katrina, when Walmart outmaneuvered FEMA. But a real solution to a credit crisis would involve a decisive assumption of responsibility not only by government and corporations, but also by individuals.

It might seem absurd not to have solutions at hand for problems that will necessarily arise due to the structure of our economic system. *People should not have to starve* or even be temporarily out of work during credit crises. Yet the apparatus for ensuring that economic stimulus reaches those who need it does not yet exist. This is why blockchain technology as a perfectly accurate system of accounting might make it possible for state resources to reach employers and citizens in need *directly*, so that the situation does not balloon into a generational social disaster. Austerity, during times of crisis, wrecks whole swaths of the population at a time and causes a more serious blowback in the long run than simply taking precautions to ensure that everyone will have the resources they need to flourish during economic 'crises'.

At no point during the operation of everyday

capitalism does the rupture between money and value become clearer than during a credit crunch, when people begin to believe that an imaginary entity has actually caused a physical Armageddon so extreme that the most valuable asset to a human being—its peers within its own social context—could be reduced to the status of absolute worthlessness. This language sounds strong, but, in letting people fall out of work and into bankruptcy, this is the message. This is not only intensely foolish in terms of the alethic perspective of time, but also a practical error predicated on the false understanding that allowing the most valuable entities in existence—the wealth-generating human elements of one's own society—to deteriorate will actually assist the long-run arithmetic progression of capital. Clearly, this is a problem even for those who would seem to be insulated from an economic downturn.

We'll end on a philological high note. The word 'finance' comes into English through the French lineage of the Latin word *finis*. We usually translate this word as 'end' and see it as a punctual moment in space and time like a 'finish' line. But English speakers have been deprived of an adequate translation of an important aspect of the origins of how this word is actually used. Cicero in the *De Finibus* injects a forgotten specter of Koine Greek into Latin: he gives us the clue that he uses the term *finis* as the Greeks use the word telos (τέλος). Many works translate the word *telos* as end, but its richer, actual meaning denotes the absolute *fulfillment* and *completion* of a thing in terms of what it is. A fulfilled, completed, or teleion (τέλειον) entity is maxed out absolutely in regard to best aspects of its essence. The technology of money well applied can at best serve as a *limited* means toward human fulfillment that must continuously be subordinated *to the human being that gives it its value in the first place.*

Money, which started out as a useful invention, has supposedly become an 'absolute' measure for all phenomena within society. But financial valuations in terms of shortsighted quantifications can never actually represent human value. For this reason, financial quantities can simply not express the fulfillment of the whole entity of the human being and society. There is potentially an enormous disjunction between a person's net worth or income and their value—even their economic value—to society.

We might now assert that the value of a fellow member of society is not merely 'intrinsic', but, when placed in a broader social context, also financial. An economy based on an essentially speculative monetary technology must evolve methods to sustain all of its members—even those who are not viewed as productive of immediate profit—during the violent credit contractions that are necessary because of the system's structure. This responsibility falls upon all members of the social network, because, whether it is acknowledged or not, the economic well being of each individual within the network affects the health of the network as a whole.

# BEFORE YOU GO:

As an independent author, reviews and word-of-mouth are the life-blood of my business. If you learned something new and enjoyed the book, consider leaving me a review on Amazon. You can do this by visiting The Money Phenomenon's product page on Amazon, scrolling down to the review section, and clicking "Write a Customer Review" You might be surprised at what a world of difference this little act of charity actually makes.

Kindle readers can access the Write a Review page by clicking this link!

**Thank you,**

Louis

www.ingramcontent.com/pod-product-compliance
Lightning Source LLC
Chambersburg PA
CBHW020604220526
45463CB00006B/2442